The Few Drops Known

poems by

F.S. Blake

Finishing Line Press
Georgetown, Kentucky

The Few Drops Known

*To Anne Blake,
a mother who deserves much more than this*

Copyright © 2021 by F.S. Blake
ISBN 978-1-64662-450-8 First Edition
All rights reserved under International and Pan-American Copyright Conventions. No part of this book may be reproduced in any manner whatsoever without written permission from the publisher, except in the case of brief quotations embodied in critical articles and reviews.

ACKNOWLEDGMENTS

O Dark Thirty: "Tug"
Line Of Advance: "Highfield, Jamaica"
Sanskrit Literary Magazine: "Savannah"
Juked Literary Magazine: "Wind Chime for Diana"
Door is a Jar: " Come Over and Listen to Sad Songs"
Jellyfish Whispers: "Quahog"

Publisher: Leah Huete de Maines
Editor: Christen Kincaid
Cover Art: Matt Burke
Author Photo: Diana Blake
Cover Design: Elizabeth Maines McCleavy

Printed in the USA on acid-free paper.
Order online: www.finishinglinepress.com
        also available on amazon.com

Author inquiries and mail orders:
Finishing Line Press
P. O. Box 1626
Georgetown, Kentucky 40324
U. S. A.

Table of Contents

With What Regular Frequency I Think of You 1

Can we let the Cosmos decide? 2

Balloon 3

Track 25 4

Tug 5

Love Song for Haiti 6

Highfield, Jamaica 8

Boca Cut 9

Figure Eight 10

Savannah 12

Equator 13

Mermaid 14

Lighthouse 15

Wind Chime for Diana 16

Handrail 17

Home Waters 18

Can we let our hearts decide? 19

Rain Song 20

Dark Wells 22

Come Over and Listen to Sad Songs 23

Prescription for the Future 24

Quahog 25

Of heroes, history, grand events, premises, myths, poems,
The few drops known must stand for oceans of the unknown,
On this beautiful, and thick-peopl'd earth, here and there
    A little specimen put on record

  —Walt Whitman, "Leaves of Grass"

With What Regular Frequency I Think of You

Moon and tides dance provocatively, and push and pull their bodies towards each other in an ancient dependable rhythm

And I watch the beach caught in the middle, as I think of you

Trains and their timetables bustle about busy citizens in large worldly capitals

I study their pace and focus as they move in a mass of importance while I fondly think of you

Astronomers plot the courses of unseen comets and share their predictions with worshippers and well-wishers, and while they all look to space I fondly think of you

Farmers time their crops and run the daily rigor of their lives based on generations of knowledge they log in their almanacs while I pause and think of you

Factory workers track their wages and slog away as human cogs in corporate machines

They punch their time cards at the start of the day while I am busy thinking of you

Great migratory flocks cross borders and trade climates driven by an unknown clock and compass

Their entire species is on the move while I sit peacefully and think of you

All the pieces of our world set in motion

Move with the simple luxury of consistency, but fail to come close to capturing

With what regular frequency I think of you.

Can we let the Cosmos decide?

Can we let the Cosmos decide?

And cast on the winds of fate the possibilities and options of outcomes innumerable

Can we leave it up to you, oh Goddess of chance, the hopes and dreams for which we have striven these long days?

Can we delegate to you the solemn task of impartiality and the heavy burden of just conclusions?

Can we trust you, oh great and powerful friend, to choose for us the best possible world from amongst a sea of sorrows?

Can we let the Cosmos decide?

And drop the reigns our weary hands have held so tightly

Can we find in you, the Great Arbiter of Fate, who will smooth our furrowed brow and take gladly the burden of our worry?

And can we at long last loose the yoke of personal will and force to finally rest in your caring arms as you pilot us to our inevitable destination?

Balloon

Caught between two eager forces
My heart looks out over a peaceful, golden hued valley
Slopes transition from undetectable to elegant curves of staggering grace
Birds chirp below
As I'm lifted to where clouds could be but aren't
Heat
Caught in fabric, lifts with molecular determination
Radiant energy of super-hot origin makes tiny pushes each one lifting my hopes to the sun
Balanced
By the well-worn wicker of a traveler's basket large enough to weigh down all ambition and saddled with the burden of compromises measured in pounds
I see beauty unrivaled
And drift in the silence known only to angels
Above cell phones and sales reports
Pulled up and weighted down
Beauty not searched for but floated to and found.

Track 25

A train car sits heavy and restless

And knows that on its ebbs it has brought countless happy reunion hugs

And on the tide a flood of goodbye tears

Caught in seas at the base of its tracks

A train car sits heavy

And impacts the gravity of the heart

As people orbit stations below rooftop constellations.

Tug

How can the smaller of two vessels be the course decider?
A taut cable linking an elephant trainer to the beast
Internal will and force can make even the seemingly impossible happen
Millions of pounds of freight
I'll get your cheap Chinese stuff delivered on time
Such a stout and powerful machine on a dumb task
What do you Tug?

Love Song for Haiti

Born fresh from beauty
Broken streets drawn from hands of angry mapmakers
Craggy asphalt spindles snake their way past lottery shops
And makeshift mechanics' stalls with stacks of used tires
Necklaces on girls as school shifts end and long winding commutes to life begin
Iron work, barrels turned to art
Banged out in back room clanking and borrowed hammer swings
Smoke in the distance
From a fire made from charcoal bought today from a market right beside the beginning of a long mountain road
Cooking a man's dinner after his long day sitting and suffering in traffic
Bogged down by simple needs snuffed out and cast aside by the choking throng
of tap taps and taxi bikes
Frozen soup of machines
Inching back to life by the building days' heat
Till night breaks
And cool Caribbean breezes wind through open streets and dogs prowl the
undersides of parked cars
Straight sheets of white celestial stars break across cloudless moon lit skies
Flowers open and hint at their smells
An insect chirps
And all the way down to the waterfront people sleep
And dream happy dreams
Of neighbors with family and good moods of pleasant conversations with
friends

Dreams content in big broad smiles and happy faces on tear-worn pillows
Dreams of the cities of relatives
Those whose momentum carried them far away to frigid climes
Huddled around ex-pat fires fueled by hard work and hope
Laboring layers below education levels for first-world wages
Sunrise breaks
And roosters sing to life the machines of the day
Struggle renews
Weighed down by the conscience of a continent.

Highfield, Jamaica

Is the beauty here just on the boundaries?
Where the ocean gives up, confronted by the weight of infinite grains
An hourglass exploded
On the inside, commerce, and the crumbling Caribbean concrete of strife and stress
Roadside shacks and the capitalist backwater of black-market necessity
Here, dark rum and bright beaches and the old woman's trash burning in a Parish beyond the rolling leafy hills
Clues to the tin-drum truth, past the Rasta phoniness of five-star reviews and
urgent tourist
relaxation
The beauty is all around, or wherever you look for it.

Boca Cut

There it sat
Between great gaping beaches
And wide yawning sand stretches
Combed over and re-combed daily for tourist satisfaction
Long rock reaches poke borders in oceans
And futile waves burst early on concrete breaks
And vacant condos wave at each other across the aisle
Great tidal breaths exhaled through pursed lips and accelerated flows take marsh water back to its ocean home
Sun rays wrap boats slicing out toward adventure
And weary fishermen stand on edge with their lines paused and frozen in bait born anticipation
Rough creases of weather and work-beaten fingertips hold hope and filament
Trigger finger waiting
Two old fishermen
One man whose years had long outpaced his ability stood dumbly looking out past waves and birds and sought out on the horizon some meaning he was missing
One whose clothes for that day must have been the same ones from the same
floor where for days he has walked around looking to find the thing he is missing
Two men with lines cast and hope submerged on open hooks
Separated from me
By the Boca Cut.

Figure Eight

Infinite grains of sand
On a long stretched-out beach
Washed clean of people
Shore sitting welcome to new waves born over the ocean's long journey
And bright moonrise canvas for night's evening parade of tides and crabs
and turtles
No need for shade cabanas and swim-up bars of tourist beach requirements
And no spots for those who watch the clock or cram forced enjoyment into
their half day mandatory beach excursion
The true luxury is simplicity
Of waves and sounds and thoughts
Complexity swept out to sea on the ebb
And spirited down the shore to some other beach not protected by our moat
and more subjected to condos and constant thoughts
Leisurely lemniscate
Our summer capital of friendships fueled by amazing food marinated in
traditions and inside jokes
Basted in tables of idle gossip and the decadence of mindless chatter
Freedom born from minutes trapped in our mobius
Or maybe the true luxury is time
Time to catch up and plan and soak in sun and warm regards
Time slowed down to wring every drop of summer
Time to change your mind or make a decision or not
Stretched and slowed like our island is on the edge of a cosmic black hole
Where rules changes and viewpoints shift
And schedules fall apart
And matter is remade
The true luxury is being
Being here on this sunny shore

Where evening breezes play opening numbers for world-class sunsets
Being with friends and family after wars have been fought
Being one of a handful of lucky people that get to see this paradise
Being happy
In our own endless Figure Eight.

Savannah

Fog hangs low on the rooftops of the city

Pressed flat on treetops

Clouds brought down to our level

Like parents kneeling to children

Fine mist tickles window sills

And buildings huddle together around the warmth of public squares

Domes and spires dance in the distance

And live oaks drip with approval

Equator

How many adventurers have you seen?
Witness to their cruel internal drive to find something new or leave something old
How, in ancient times, did you mark their arrival or make your boundaries known?
I imagine so many died just to cross you, and those that didn't suffered discomforts unlimited
But I, on my adventure, high above the clouds, slept peacefully as our plane sliced right through you
The only indication some spotty turbulence that briefly halted our beverage
service.

Like a rumble strip on the highway, I bounced across your line and wandered into lanes of African landscapes and smells
A new set of southern hemisphere stars the backdrop of a next act to unfold across a vast new continents
Is it an injustice to your stature the ease with which I crossed you?
Left behind is everything I've known of clockwise spirals and seasons' rhythms
And gone is half the world, a new half now to explore.

Mermaid

Captain came back
And in feeble earth bound reality
Waved his arms and beckoned all who would listen
His attempt to recount
Stories of beauty and grace
Of solitudes pierced
Of mysteries revealed
And of love
He tried to explain
But his words could never portray
The mermaid elegance
And the leisure of her love
He tried to write instead
But his human pen shook and stumbled
When it sought to paint the depths of her eyes
And the curves of her body
At every try
The Captain who in his youth had commanded vast fleets and noble charters
Could not communicate one word of his Mermaid's beauty
Until one night
Alone, in a deep dark rum stare into a gilded mirror
He heard himself whisper
"Her hair."

Lighthouse

Monument to obsolescence
Shining broad beam in a world of GPS accuracy
A bygone crucial alert reduced to quaint backdrop
No more keeper or urgent mission
Beacon won't function and birds have taken over
Thanks for what you did,
but your one-dimensional mission is replaced at sea
by stars we'll never plot.

Wind Chime for Diana

Notes in the open
Play a tune for the first joke she told me
And sing a song about the movies she took me to when I was a child who appreciated being included
Every beautiful sound
Wrung from the wind and played in random orders that mimic the orchestra of angels
Crescendo on the breeze
And my aunt who passed away on my mind
She loved the simple beauty of the wind chime
Reflected its grace
And on this breezy afternoon I listen to its playlist
Sitting next to the daughter who now has the notes of her name flowing through her
Catching sounds, not making them.

Handrail

An old wooden handrail
Wound inside the building that has seen hundreds of years
Of visitors and conspirators and revolutionaries and artists
And the marble steps showed wear from the feet of families
Gas lamps faded to electric progress at the hand of workers
Owners came and went in tides of capital hopes
The thick oak railing
With its deep tones and marbled color
Sturdy wood polished
Handsome in its working
Lived through it all mostly unnoticed
But gave support to them all.

Home Waters

Known through instinct and memory
Knowledge gained from countless passes
Curves anticipated and softly navigated with smooth and steady hands of confidence
Every ripple foreseen
And hidden danger easily avoided
Gliding without fear or the dogged-down feelings that come from taking new paths or cutting new avenues
Experiencing the known like replaying a song you love
Or like running your hands over the same curve of the same woman
There is no greater feeling than being free to move
In your own
Home waters.

Can we let our hearts decide?

Can we let our hearts decide?

And cast on the seas of love

The inevitability and singularity of our future

Can we leave to you, Oh passion angel

The facts and figures we have calculated on short nights?

Can we ask of you, the solemn favor of binding lives together?

Can we trust you, our beautiful and graceful friend

To remove from our eyes the complications behind our own kisses and connections

And just let our hearts decide

To grab the worn wooden ship's wheel of life

And can we find in your kind face

The knowing smile of passion and the playful wink of desire

And at long last cede control and trust our wild hearts to dodge the traps of chance

And carry us into each other's arms forever.

Rain Song

The tears of unseen clouds trickle down in cautious increments
And strengthen and fade tied to an unknown cadence

I long for pattern rain!

And the predictable showtimes of more southern climes

Of equatorial consistency

And deep green jungle familiarity

I long for the rain you can set your watch to

That pours with the regularity of a Colorado mountain afternoon soak
Or that comes at the same time every year to honor the faithful farmer

I curse this rain!

That catches suburban shoppers unaware
And traps its victims in parking lots and public spaces

Oh fickle rain!

That comes and goes on the whims of its own barometer

You tread meek landscapes and hint at your fierce older relatives

 Silly and stressful rain!

Give way

And run your droplets back to puddles and rivers

Return you to your origin

The one fine molecule of water

Dissemble ye few drops known

Into the larger consciousness
And disappear your random rains

Come back to us, O storms
On the hour
And announce your arrival with great thunderous claps and furious bolts

We bid you greetings at your appointed time and welcome you to serve our purposes

We celebrate you, O annual downpours

As we bend our worlds to manipulate your powers and protect ourselves from your terrifying might.

Dark Wells

Unbearable goddamned anger

Flowing through my violent pen held in the pursed fingers of a shaking hand

Ink drawn from dark wells

Brought up from deep beneath the sleeping Earth

And put to crisp paper as an appeasement offering or ancient letting of blood.

Come Over and Listen to Sad Songs

Rest in my arms and let fly the rusty hinges of our hearts

Sit deeply

And let the blue notes and soulful cries wash over our day-weary bodies and cover us in the sorrows of their songwriters

Let's trade for a moment the problems we know so well we can draw their complex profiles from memory

And try on new layers of unfamiliar sadness

And take for a test drive other worries whose finer points and issues we only just begin to see

Let's swap our stresses for the struggles of the heartbroken or the melancholy of the poor artists

Let us drink deeply of their experience and allow their moods to implant themselves in us on purpose

Our self-chosen torture

With tears on deck

And old wounds rubbed anew

Come over and listen to sad songs

As we bask in beautiful minor keys

And cry for our broken parts or lives we never knew.

Prescription for the Future

Go see a sunrise she said
And I sat in the cool morning air and saw the horizon hinted at by colors
One last star in the sky
Dark clouds prepping for rainbows
Buildings born to block
And our stage slowly turned on by arcing rays returning
And eventually the entire world is visible
Before the sun even breaks the plane
Burning away years of pain
And writing a prescription for the future.

Quahog

Buried in sand and rock and ocean for years
My solitude a trickle of salty tears

Hidden from sight and love
Hard shell protects

My life gone in a flash like gunpowder
Don't take me for your chowder.

F.S. Blake is a writer and Bronze Star decorated U.S. Army veteran. His poetry has been published in such literary journals as *As You Were, O-Dark-Thirty,* and *Wrath-Bearing Tree*. He has published two chapbooks of poetry including work related to war and military service: *Terminal Leave* (2018) and *Above the Gold Fields* (2019), each from Finishing Line Press. He was nominated for a Pushcart Prize in 2018. For more information about his writing, visit: www.fsblake.com.

www.ingramcontent.com/pod-product-compliance
Lightning Source LLC
LaVergne TN
LVHW041517070426
835507LV00012B/1643